AMAZING SCIENCE

AMAZING LIGHT

Sally Hewitt

 Crabtree Publishing Company
www.crabtreebooks.com

Crabtree Publishing Company
www.crabtreebooks.com

Editors: L. Michelle Nielsen, Michael Hodge
Senior Editor: Joyce Bentley
Senior Design Manager: Rosamund Saunders
Designer: Tall Tree

Photo Credits: Llianski/Alamy: p. 22; Paul Ridsdale/Alamy: p.23; D. Boone/Corbis: p. 6; Pat Doyle/Corbis: p. 21; Craig Tuttle/Corbis: p. 18; Gary Bell/Getty Images: p. 11; Steve Bloom/Getty Images; p. 12; Charles Bowman/Getty Images: p. 16; Bruno Ehrs/Getty Images: p. 7; Macduff Everton/Getty Images: p. 10; Didier Givois/Getty Images: p. 27; Jeff Hunter/Getty Images: cover, p. 14; Jan Tove Johansson/Getty Images: p. 8; Laurie & Charles/Getty Images: p. 17; Rob Melnychuk/Getty Images: p. 25; Eric Meola/Getty Images: p. 26; Laurence Monneret/Getty Images: p. 13; Manfred Rutz/Getty Images: p. 3, p. 19; Gregor Schuster/Getty Images: p. 24; Larry Tackett/Getty Images: p. 20; Stuart Westmoreland/Getty Images: p. 9; Cordelia Molloy/Science Photo Library p.15.

Activity & illustrations: Shakespeare Squared pp. 28-29.

Cover: Fireworks explode in the night sky.

Title page: A girl blows bubbles. A rainbow of color can be seen on the bubbles' surface.

Library and Archives Canada Cataloguing in Publication

Hewitt, Sally, 1949-
    Amazing light / Sally Hewitt.

(Amazing science)
Includes index.
ISBN 978-0-7787-3612-7 (bound)
ISBN 978-0-7787-3626-4 (pbk.)

    1. Light--Juvenile literature. 2. Optics--Juvenile literature.
I. Title. II. Series: Hewitt, Sally, 1949- . Amazing science.

QC360.H49 2007   j535   C2007-904309-7

Library of Congress Cataloging-in-Publication Data

Hewitt, Sally, 1949-
    Amazing light / Sally Hewitt.
        p. cm. -- (Amazing science)
    Includes index.
    ISBN-13: 978-0-7787-3612-7 (rlb)
    ISBN-10: 0-7787-3612-1 (rlb)
    ISBN-13: 978-0-7787-3626-4 (pb)
    ISBN-10: 0-7787-3626-1 (pb)
    1. Light--Juvenile literature. 2. Light--Experiments--Juvenile literature.
I. Title. II. Series.

QC360.H487 2008
535--dc22
                                    2007027425

Crabtree Publishing Company
www.crabtreebooks.com   1-800-387-7650

Printed in China/082011/FC20110523

Published in Canada
Crabtree Publishing
616 Welland Ave.
St. Catharines, ON
L2M 5V6

Published in the United States
Crabtree Publishing
PMB 59051
350 Fifth Avenue, 59th Floor
New York, New York 10118

Contents

Amazing light   6

Night   8

No light   10

How we see   12

Glowing light   14

Rays and shadows   16

Rainbows   18

Seeing colors   20

Reflections   22

Sparkling and shiny   24

Clouds and sunshine   26

A rainbow all your own!   28

Glossary   30

Index   32

Amazing light

The sun is a huge ball of burning gas that is far away in space. It is so bright that it can be seen on Earth.

The sun **lights** up the world during the day.

Earth spins around in space. It is daytime on the part of Earth that is facing the sun.

Day begins at sunrise and ends at sunset.

WARNING!

Never look at the sun. Its strong light can hurt your **eyes***.*

SCIENCE WORDS: light gas sun

Night

The moon is made of rock and does not give off light of its own. Moonlight is really sunlight lighting up the moon.

It is **night** in a place on Earth when that part of Earth is turned away from the sun.

It is **dark** at night. People cannot see well at night because they need light to see things clearly.

YOUR TURN!

What can you see in a dark room? Shine a flashlight around the room. What can you see now?

Street lamps and headlights light up dark streets at night.

SCIENCE WORDS: **moon night dark**

No light

You cannot see anything deep inside a cave because there is no light. You need lanterns or flashlights to help you see.

There is no light far beneath the sea or at the bottom of a deep lake.

Some animals that live in these dark places have small eyes or no eyes, and they use other ways to find their way around.

YOUR TURN!

Make a corner of your bedroom as dark as you can. How can you keep out the light?

A cave crayfish finds its way in the dark with long **feelers**.

SCIENCE WORDS: dark feelers

How we see

Some animals have great eyesight. An eagle can see a mouse moving from over half a mile (one kilometer) away.

Rays of light **bounce** off of the things around us and go into our eyes, allowing us to see.

When you **shut** your eyes, your eyelids keep out light, and you cannot see what is around you.

YOUR TURN!

Look at your eyes in a **mirror**. Can you see black circles? They are holes called **pupils** that let light into your eyes.

You shut your eyes when you are asleep.

SCIENCE WORDS: eyes pupil shut

Glowing light

Fireworks explode and **glow** when gunpowder inside the fireworks is set on fire. They light up the dark night sky.

It would be difficult to see fireworks glowing in daylight.

When you turn on a lightbulb, a thin wire inside the bulb gets very **hot**.

The hot wire glows and gives out light.

YOUR TURN!

Can you think of something else that glows with heat and gives out light?

Rays and shadows

Sunlight shines between the trunks and branches of trees in a forest. It brightens up the dark forest with stripes of light.

Light comes from the sun in straight lines called rays.

Rays of sunlight cannot shine through something solid like a person, so a person's shape makes a shadow.

YOUR TURN!

Jump and dance outside on a sunny day. Watch your shadow dance along with you.

A shadow is the dark place where sun cannot shine.

Rainbows

A rainbow is an arch of light. It appears when sunlight shines through drops of water and splits into seven colors.

Rainbow colors are red, orange, yellow, green, light blue, dark blue, and purple.

On a sunny day, you see rainbows form on the outsides of bubbles.

Sunlight shines on bubbles to reveal rainbows.

YOUR TURN!

Blow bubbles outside on a sunny day. Look for the rainbow colors in the bubbles.

SCIENCE WORDS: rainbow color

Seeing colors

There are millions of different colors to see in the world. Colorful birds and flowers brighten up the rainforest.

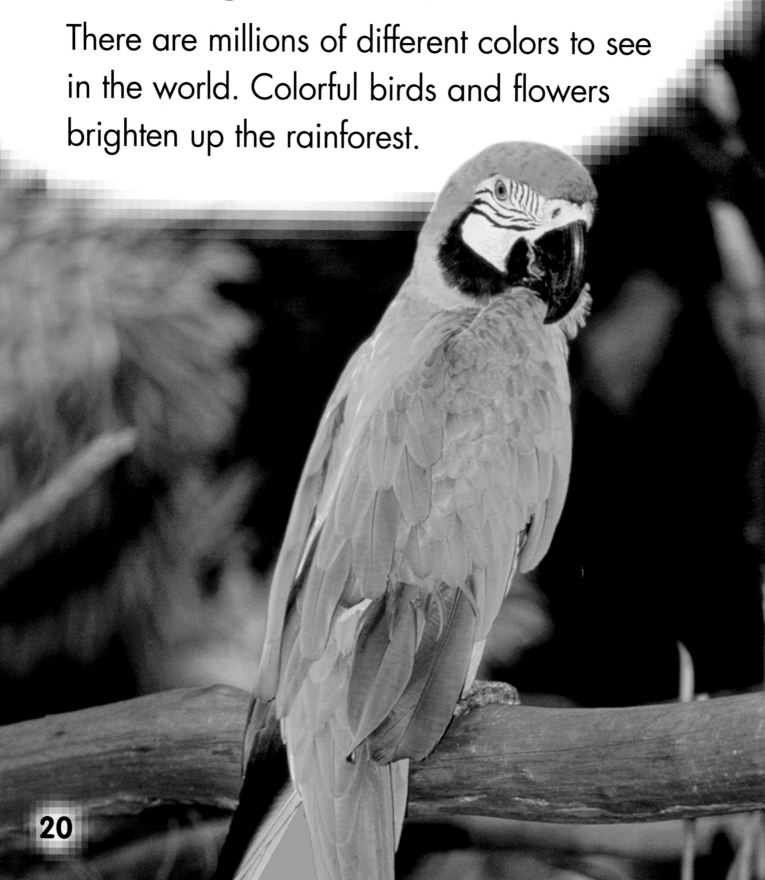

The parrot looks blue because blue light bounces off of it into your eyes, while the other colors are **absorbed**.

One of the kittens below looks white because all of the colors of light bounce off of its fur.

YOUR TURN!

See how many different colors you can make by mixing red, yellow, and blue paints together.

The other kitten looks black because its fur absorbs all of the colors.

SCIENCE WORDS: bounce absorbs

21

Reflections

Light bounces off of mirrors because they are **smooth** and **shiny**. We see **reflections** in mirrors.

Light shining from around you onto a mirror is reflected back, and you see yourself.

Cyclists often have **reflectors** on their bicycles and wear reflective clothing so that they can be seen by drivers in the dark.

When car headlights bounce off of reflectors, the reflectors shine in the dark.

YOUR TURN!

Write your name and look at it in the mirror. How does it look different?

Sparkling and shiny

The sea reflects light on a sunny and breezy day. The breeze blows the sea and makes it **ripple**.

Sunlight bounces off of ripples in all directions, and we see **sparkles**.

Light shining on a smooth metal surface, such as a stainless-steel kettle, makes the surface look shiny.

Light bounces off of smooth surfaces and makes them shine.

YOUR TURN!

Make a collection of smooth, shiny things. Put them in the light to see how they shine.

SCIENCE WORDS: **ripple   sparkle   smooth**

Clouds and sunshine

On a cloudy day, **clouds** cover Earth like a blanket. On some cloudy days, the sun cannot be seen.

Clouds let only some sunlight shine through them.

The sun shines brightly when there are no clouds, so people wear sunglasses to **protect** their eyes.

YOUR TURN!

Shine a flashlight through a tissue, cellophane, paper, and thick cardboard. What happens to the light?

Dark lenses keep some sunlight out of our eyes.

SCIENCE WORDS: **clouds protect shine**

A rainbow all your own!

Do this activity on a sunny day. See if you can make the colors of a rainbow appear on a piece of paper.

What you need

- water
- sunlight
- glass jar
- small mirror
- white piece of paper

1. Take the glass jar and fill it with water. Only fill it about three-quarters of the way. Make sure there is some extra space at the top.

2. Place the small mirror in the jar of water. Let the mirror lean against the side of the jar so that the mirror is at an angle.

3. Place your jar in a position so that the sun is shining on it. Make sure that sunlight is hitting the mirror.

4. Hold the white sheet of paper at an angle in front of the mirror. The paper should be held slightly above the mirror so that the reflection is on the paper. Move the paper around until you see the magnificent colors of the rainbow on it!

What you will see:

The sunlight that shines on us is made of seven different colors. These colors are red, orange, yellow, green, blue, indigo, and violet. By placing the mirror in the water, you have made a prism. A prism is something that separates the different colors from light. This is why you see rainbows when it rains. The rain drops are acting like little prisms. As sunlight shines through the rain drops, the light is separated, and a rainbow is created.

Glossary

absorb When something disappears into something else.

bounce To hit something and jump back off of it quickly.

cloud Millions of tiny drops of water that make a mist in the sky.

color Red, orange, yellow, green, light blue, dark blue, and purple are the colors of light that we see around us.

dark It is dark when there is no light. We cannot see in the dark.

day It is day in the part of the world that is facing the sun.

eyes The parts of your body that you see with.

feelers Some animals have feelers, such as antennae, that tell them what is happening around them.

glow When some things get very hot they glow and give off light.

hot Things get hot when they are heated. Hot is the opposite of cold.

light The sun, candles, and lamps give off light. We need light to see.

mirror A flat, shiny surface in which we can see our reflections.

moon A ball of rock in space. We see sunlight shining on it at night.

night   It is night in the part of the world that is facing away from the sun.

protect   To make sure things or people do not come to harm. Sunglasses protect your eyes from the sun.

pupil   The black hole in the center of an eye that lets in light.

rainbow   An arch of colored light in the sky.

rays   Light travels in straight lines called rays.

reflection   The picture of yourself that you see in a mirror or any shiny surface.

reflectors   Reflectors are materials that light bounces off of. They glow in the dark.

ripple   A series of waves that appear when something touches a pool of water.

shadow   A dark place where light cannot shine. When sunlight cannot shine through a solid object, a shadow is made.

shiny   Something with a smooth surface that reflects light is shiny.

shut   The opposite of open. You shut your eyes to keep out the light.

smooth   The opposite of rough. A smooth surface is flat and even.

sparkle   To reflect light in bright flashes.

sun   A giant ball of burning gas in space.

Index

black 13, 21
blue 19, 21, 29, 30

color 18, 19, 20, 21, 29,
  30, 31

dark 9, 11, 14, 16, 17, 23,
  30, 31
day 7, 17, 19, 24, 26, 30
daylight 15

eyes, eyesight 7, 11, 12, 13,
  21, 27, 30, 31

gas 6
green 19, 29, 30

headlights 9, 23
heat 15, 30

light bulb 15

mirror 13, 22, 23, 28,
  29, 30
moon 8, 30
moonlight 8

night 8, 9, 14, 30, 31

orange 19, 29, 30

pupil 13, 31
purple 19, 30

rainbow 18, 19, 28, 29, 31
rays 13, 16, 17, 31
red 19, 21, 29, 30
reflection 22, 23, 29, 30, 31
reflectors 23, 31

shadows 16, 17, 31
shine 9, 16, 17, 19, 23,
  25, 31
shiny 22, 25, 31
smooth 22, 25, 31
sparkle 24, 25, 31
sun 6, 7, 9, 17, 26, 29,
  30, 31
sunglasses 27, 31
sunlight 9, 16, 17, 18, 19,
  26, 27, 28, 29, 31
sunny 17, 19, 24, 28

white 21

yellow 19, 21, 29, 30